MATHS PLUS
FROM HEINEMANN

USING MATHS WITH

Language Book 1

for 7-9 year olds

apex

bisect

clockwise

dodecahedron

outcomes

equally likely

fraction

$\frac{1}{2}$

STEVE MILLS • HILARY KOLL

Heinemann

Heinemann Educational Publishers
Halley Court, Jordan Hill, Oxford, OX2 8EJ
a division of Reed Educational and Professional Publishing Ltd

Heinemann is a registered trademark of Reed Educational and Professional
Publishing Ltd

OXFORD   MELBOURNE   AUCKLAND
CHICAGO   PORTSMOUTH (NH)   IBADAN
GABORONE   JOHANNESBURG   BLANTYRE

First published 1999

04 03 02 01 00
10 9 8 7 6 5 4 3

Language Book 1   ISBN 0 435 02567 8
(pack of 6)   ISBN 0 435 02569 4

Designed and illustrated by Artistix
Printed and bound in Great Britain

Contents

Properties of number

number, set, digit, numeral, column, whole number, fraction, number line, odd
number, even number, abacus, negative number, positive number

1 Which is the largest **number** in this **set**? 17 12 21 9 5

2 How many **digits** does each of these **numbers** have?
   a) 23   **b)** 5   **c)** 17   **d)** 300   **e)** 1287

3 Write the **number** twelve as a **numeral**.

4 Draw two **columns** and sort these **numbers** into **whole
   numbers** and **fractions**.

7	$\frac{1}{2}$	52	6	0	$\frac{1}{4}$	42	$\frac{3}{4}$	18	$\frac{7}{8}$

5 Draw a **number line** from 0 to 10 and mark on these **whole
   numbers**.
   9   4   7   1   3

6 On your **number line**, colour the **odd numbers** red and the
   even numbers blue.

7 What **number** is shown on this **abacus**?
   Draw five more of your own and write the
   numbers each abacus shows.

8 Choose three different **digits**. Arrange them in as many different
   ways as you can into new three-digit numbers. Put these
   numbers in order, with the smallest first.

9 Draw a **number line** from −10 to +10 showing **negative** and
   positive numbers.

10 Using your **number line** with **negative** and **positive
   numbers**, say if these are true or false:
   a) −7 is smaller than −6   **b)** 4 is greater than −4
   c) −1 is smaller than −2
   Write some sentences like these of your own. Now write
   whether they are true or false.

Place value and ordering

value, number, digit, figure, numeral, unit, equals, equivalent, abacus, approximation, rounding, total, plus, difference, sum, decimal, zero

1 What is the **value** of the 6 in 163?

2 Which of these numbers is 'four hundred and four'?
   44   4004   440   404

3 Which of the **digits** in this number is the hundreds digit? 4852

4 Which three of these **numbers** have a 6 as the tens digit?
   60   236   689   696   168   4362

5 Choose three different **digits**. Arrange them in as many different ways as you can into new three-**figure** numbers. Write these **numbers** as **numerals** and in words.

6 Which statement is true?
   a) 7 tens and 5 **units equals** 705
   b) 7 hundreds and 5 **units** is **equivalent** to 750
   c) 7 tens and 5 **units** is **equivalent** to 750
   d) 7 tens and 5 **units** is **equivalent** to 75

7 What **number** is shown on this **abacus**? Draw five more of your own and write the numbers each abacus shows.

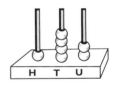

8 Make an **approximation** by **rounding** these numbers to the nearest ten.
   49   61   74   98   37   23

9 Do these quickly:
   a) find the **total** of 10 and 9
   b) 100 **plus** 1
   c) find the **difference** between 299 and 200
   d) the **sum** of 1 and 999

10 Write some **decimals** that are larger than **zero** but smaller than one.

3 Addition and subtraction

addition, subtraction, plus, difference, minus, increasing, decreasing, approximation, total, sum

1 Copy and complete this sentence, '**Addition** means ...'.

2 Write some other words that mean **addition**.

3 Copy and complete this sentence, '**Subtraction** means ...'.

4 Write some other words that mean **subtraction**.

5 True or false?
   a) 10 **subtract** 7 makes 17   **b)** 6 **plus** 4 equals 10
   c) the **difference** between 9 and 5 is 4   **d)** 16 **minus** 7 equals 9

6 Make up some **addition** sums that give the answer 24.

7 Which statement is true?
   a) when we add things together, we are **increasing** the number of things
   b) when we add things together, we are **decreasing** the number of things
   c) when we add things together, we make an **approximation** of the number of things

8 Make up a story for each of these **addition** and **subtraction** facts. A story has been written for the first one.

   $7 - 6 = 1$ I made 7 cakes for my friends. My 6 friends came for tea and they ate 1 each. There was 1 cake left for me.

   $8 + 6 = 14$ $25 + 20 = 45$ $16 - 8 = 8$ $12 + 8 + 4 = 24$

9 Answer these:
   a) add 12 and 6   **b)** 7 **plus** 8   **c)** find the **total** of 12 and 6
   d) find the **difference** between 20 and 10
   e) the **sum** of 3 and 9

10 Make up some **subtraction** questions that give the answer 10.

Multiplication and division

multiplication, division, product, number, remainder

1 Copy and complete this sentence, '**Multiplication** means …'.

2 Which of these words could mean **multiplication**?
   plus   times   share   lots of   minus   sum
   multiplied by   groups of

3 Copy and complete this sentence, '**Division** means …'.

4 Which of these words could mean **division**?
   plus   times   share   lots of   minus   sum
   divided by   groups of

5 True or false?
   a) 10 times 7 makes 70   **b)** 6 multiplied by 4 equals 32
   c) 12 divided by 4 is 3   **d)** 16 shared between 2 equals 8

6 Make up some **multiplication** questions that give the
   answer 24.

7 Write down what **product** means in maths.

8 Make up a story for each of these **number** facts. A story has
   been written for the first one.

   $2 \times 4 = 8$ My 2 dogs have 4 legs each, so they have 8 legs
                     altogether.

   $8 \times 2 = 16$ $4 \times 5 = 20$ $3 \times 4 = 12$ $6 \times 3 = 18$

9 Answer these:
   a) divide 12 by 2   **b)** 24 shared between 8
   c) find the **product** of 5 and 6   **d)** 20 times 10

10 Copy and complete this sentence, '12 divided by 5 has a
    remainder of …'.
    Make up some **division** questions that all have a remainder.

3 Fractions

fraction, half, number, quarter, whole number, sixth, third, eighth, fifth

1 Copy and complete this sentence, 'A **fraction** is ...'.

2 What is a **half**? How can you write a half using **numbers**?

3 Draw some squares in your book. Colour a **half** of each one so they all look different. What **fraction** is not coloured in each square?

4 What is a **quarter**? How can you write a quarter using **numbers**?

5 Draw some squares in your book. Colour a **quarter** of each one so they all look different. What **fraction** is not coloured in each square?

6 Which statement is true?
   a) three **quarters** is written as $\frac{4}{3}$
   b) two **quarters** make a **half**
   c) a **half** is smaller than a **quarter**

7 What **fraction** of crosses are in the ring? What fraction is not in the ring?

8 Find a **half** of each of these **whole numbers**: 8 6 10 20 30

9 True or false?
   a) A **sixth** is written as $\frac{1}{2}$.   **b)** A **third** is written as $\frac{3}{4}$.
   c) An **eighth** is written as $\frac{1}{8}$.   **d)** A **fifth** is written as $\frac{5}{1}$.

10 Write some sentences like these of your own. Now write whether they are true or false.

Decimals

decimal, decimal point, half, fraction, metre, tenth, column, set, digit, centimetre

1 Copy and complete this sentence, 'A **decimal** is ...'.

2 Write a number with a **decimal point** in it.

3 What is a **half**? Write a half as a **fraction** and as a **decimal**.

4 Write these numbers as **decimals**:
   a) two and a half **metres**   **b)** half a **metre**
   c) four and a half **metres**   **d)** ten and a half **metres**

5 Write four different **decimals** that have a 3 in the **tenths column**.

6 Draw ten buttons.

   Colour seven **tenths** of the **set** of buttons in blue.
   Write this as a **decimal**.

7 What numbers can you make with these **digits** and a **decimal point**?

   Write the numbers you make in order, with the smallest first.

8 How many **centimetres** are there in 1.25 **metres**?

9 A magazine costs £2. A book costs £4.20. A pencil case costs 50p.
   If you bought two of these items, how much could you spend?

10 Write some **decimals** that are larger than 1 but smaller than 2.

3 Number patterns and algebra

sequence, whole number, odd number, negative number, even number, difference, number, number line, positive number, value, multiplication

1 Continue this **sequence:**   1, 3, 5, 7, 9, ...

2 List all the **whole numbers** from 20 to 30. Which of these are **odd numbers?**

3 When you multiply any **whole number** by 2 you will always get:
a) an **odd number**   **b)** a **negative number**
c) an **even number**

4 Find the **difference** between each of the **numbers** in this **sequence:**   3, 7, 11, 15, 19

5 Make up a **sequence** with a **difference** of 5 between each of the **numbers.**

6 Draw a **number line** from −10 to 10, with **positive numbers** and **negative numbers** on it. Use the number line to continue this **sequence:**   7, 5, 3, 1, ...

7 The rule for finding the next **number** in this **sequence** is 'multiply by 2 and add 1'.
Find the next three numbers in this sequence: 1, 3, 7, ...
Write one thing you notice about the numbers in this sequence.

8 This snake has a **sequence** written inside it. Describe the sequence in words.

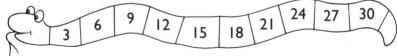

Draw a sequence snake and write your own sequence with **positive** and **negative numbers** in it. Describe the sequence.

9 Find the **values** of the missing **numbers:**
a) 8 + ... = 15   **b)** 19 − ... = 8   **c)** 4 − ... = −1

10 Make up some **multiplication** questions with missing **numbers.**

Names of two-dimensional shapes

square, rectangle, hexagon, pentagon, octagon, triangle, vertex

3

1 Copy and complete this sentence, 'A **square** is ...'.

2 Draw three different **rectangles** in your book.

3 What is the difference between a **square** and a **rectangle**?

4 Choose the correct name for each shape from the names in the box.

| rectangle | circle | square | triangle | semicircle |

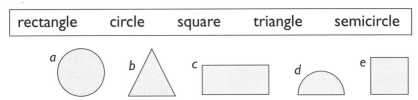

5 What is a **hexagon**?

6 Draw two different **hexagons**.

7 Which statement is true?
   a) a **hexagon** has five sides **b)** a **pentagon** is a star shape
   c) an **octagon** has six sides **d)** a **triangle** always has three sides

8 Which of these shapes are **triangles**?

9 What is a **vertex**? Write the names of five flat shapes and how many vertices they have.

10 Which of these shapes are **pentagons**?

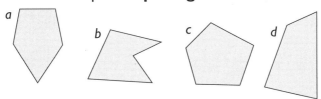

3 Properties of two-dimensional shapes

length, square, angle, rectangle, hexagon, vertex, line of symmetry, reflective symmetry, column, right-angle, Venn diagram, pentagon, right-angled triangle

1. What is special about the **length** of the sides of a **square**?

2. Write down how many **angles** a **rectangle** has and what these angles are called.

3. Draw a **hexagon** and an arrow pointing to a **vertex** on it. How many vertices does a hexagon have?

4. How many **lines of symmetry** does a **square** have?

5. Which of these shapes have **reflective symmetry**?

6. Write down four things in your classroom that have **reflective symmetry**.

7. Draw three **columns** and sort out these shapes:
   a) shapes with no **right-angles**
   b) shapes with one **right-angle**
   c) shapes with more than one **right-angle**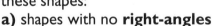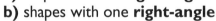

8. Copy this **Venn diagram** and put the shapes in question seven into the correct places.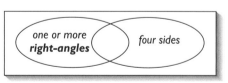

9. True or false?
   a) a **pentagon** has six sides   b) a **vertex** is a corner of a shape
   c) a **right-angled triangle** has three right-angles

10. Draw a picture of a house using one **pentagon**, four **squares** and two **rectangles**. Mark on the house all the **right-angles** you can see.

Circles

circle, semicircle, half, edge, solid shape, face, cube, cone, cuboid, cylinder, reflective symmetry, line of symmetry, oval, turn, right-angle, half turn, quarter turn, compass

3

1 Copy and complete this sentence, 'A **circle** is ...'.

2 True or false?
   a) a **semicircle** is **half** a **circle**   **b)** a **circle** has one **edge**

3 Which of these **solid shapes** has at least one **face** that is a
   circle?   **cube**   **cone**   **cuboid**   **cylinder**

4 Which of the objects below has at
   least one **face** that is a **circle**?

   List any other objects you
   can see with at least one
   face that is a circle.

   pencil case   *clock*   *door*

5 Find a circular lid. Draw around it and cut out a **circle**.
   How many different ways can you fold the **circle** in **half**?
   Does a circle have **reflective symmetry**?

6 Cut the **circle** in **half** to make a **semicircle**. How many
   different ways can you fold the semicircle in half?
   How many **lines of symmetry** does a semicircle have?

7 Look at this pattern.
   How many **ovals** are there?
   How many **circles** are there?
   How many **semicircles** are there?

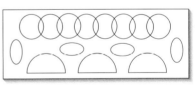

8 Make up a pattern using **ovals**, **circles** and **semicircles**.

9 **a)** If you **turn** a full **circle**, how many **right-angles** do you turn?
   b) If you **turn** a **half turn**, how many **right-angles** do you turn?
   c) If you **turn** a **quarter turn**, how many **right-angles** do you
      turn?

10 Draw a **compass**. Show the main compass points in a **circle**.

3 Names of three-dimensional shapes

solid shape, cone, cylinder, sphere, cuboid, cube, pyramid, hemisphere, rectangular prism, prism, triangular prism

1 Copy and complete this sentence, 'A **solid shape** is ...'.

2 Choose the correct name for each **solid shape** from the names in the box.

cone	cylinder	sphere	cuboid

a   *b*   *c*   *d*

3 Draw pictures of three different **cuboids**. What is another name for a cuboid?

4 Name something that is shaped like a **cube**.

5 What is a **pyramid**? Can you draw one?

6 Write down anything you can see around you that is shaped like:
   cone   cylinder   sphere   cuboid
   (list them like this: **sphere** – ball)

7 What is the Northern **Hemisphere**?

8 Draw a picture of a **hemisphere**.

9 Draw a shape person, using the following shapes:
   a) a **cone** for a hat   **b)** a **sphere** for a face
   c) a **cuboid** for a body   **d) cylinders** for arms and legs
   e) hemispheres for feet
   Draw some more shape people or animals. Write the names of the shapes you use.

10 Here is a picture of a **rectangular prism**. What is a prism? Draw a picture of a **triangular prism**. Can you think of anything in real life that is the shape of a triangular prism?

Properties of three-dimensional shapes

face, cube, edge, cuboid, solid shape, hemisphere, sphere, cone, cylinder, Carroll diagram, pyramid

1 What shape are the **faces** of a **cube**?

2 Copy and complete this sentence, 'An **edge** is ...'.

3 How many **faces** and **edges** does a **cuboid** have?

4 Name these **solid shapes**. Which of the shapes has only straight **edges**?

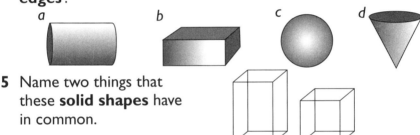

a   b   c   d

5 Name two things that these **solid shapes** have in common.

6 True or false?
   a) Two **hemispheres** that are the same size can be joined to make a **sphere**.
   b) A **cone** has only flat **faces**.
   c) A **cylinder** has only straight **edges**.

7 Which **solid shape** has only one **face** and no **edges**?

8 Sort these **solid shapes** and complete the **Carroll diagram**.
   cone   cuboid
   cube   sphere

Right-angles	No right-angles

9 Find some **pyramids** to look at. Write down what you notice about the shape of most of the **faces**. How many faces on the pyramid are *not* this shape?

10 Write a list of any **solid shapes** you can see around you which have curved **edges**.

3 Length

length, height, weight, distance, depth, area, capacity, breadth, width, span, pace, palm, distance, centimetre, height, width, metre, vertical, horizontal, diagonal

1 Copy and complete this sentence, '**Length** means ...'.

2 Which of these lines has the longest **length**?

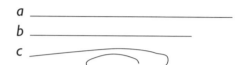

    a _____

    b _____

    c

3 Which of these words are lengths? **height**   **weight**
   distance   **depth**   **area**   **capacity**   **breadth**   **width**

4 True or false?
   a) A **span** is the measurement between your elbow and fingertip.
   b) A **pace** is the measurement between your toe and heel.
   c) A **palm** is the measurement across your hand with fingers
      together.

5 Find the **distance** from one end of your table to the other.
Measure this **length** using **palms**, **spans** and **centimetres**.

6 What is the **height** of this table?

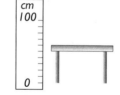

7 Draw a picture of a house.
Make the **width** of the house
5 **centimetres**.

8 How many **centimetres** make one **metre**?

9 This pattern is made up of **vertical**,
horizontal and **diagonal lines**.
Measure these lines in **centimetres**.

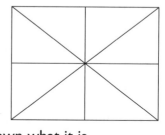

10 Measure the length of different things
in your classroom using **centimetres**
and **metres**. Find something that
measures about 2 metres and write down what it is.

Time

time, clockwise, half, time, unit, quarter, half turn, angle

1 What **time** does this clock show?

2 Sketch this clock and draw an arrow
   to show which way is **clockwise**.

3 What number is the long hand pointing to if the clock is showing
   half past two?

4 Copy and complete this sentence, 'We measure the passing of
   time in **units** like ...'.

5 How many minutes are there in:
   a) one hour?   **b) half** an hour?
   c) quarter of an hour?   **d)** three **quarters** of an hour?

6 What time will this clock show if the
   long hand moves a **half turn clockwise**?

7 Look at the **angles** between the hands on these clocks.
   The clocks all have something in common. Write down what it is.

   Draw another clock that has the same thing in common.

8 How would you write these **times** on a digital clock?
   a) four o'clock   **b) half** past three
   c) quarter past nine   **d) quarter** to two

9 **a)** A baby girl spends **half** the day asleep, how many hours is this?
   b) Mike spends one **quarter** of the day watching TV, how many
   hours is this?

10 How many hours are you at school in one day? In one week?

Mass and capacity

weight, scales, gram, kilogram, capacity, cylinder, litre, millilitre, depth, area

1 Copy and complete this sentence, '**Weight** means ...'.

2 Which of these pairs of **scales** is correct?

3 How many **grams** are there in 1 **kilogram**?

4 Which of these pairs of **scales** is correct?

 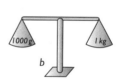 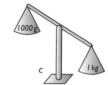

5 Use **scales** to find your weight. Write it in **kilograms**.

6 Copy and complete this sentence, '**Capacity** means ...'.

7 Draw a picture of a **cylinder**. If it holds 2 **litres** when it is full, mark where 1 litre would reach and where 0.5 litres would reach.

8 Which of these words can we use when we are finding the **capacity** of something?
weight   cylinder   litre   gram   millilitre   depth   area

9 Draw 1 **litre** of water in each of these **cylinders**. Each cylinder holds 2 litres when full.

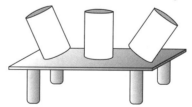

10 True or false?
   a) A **litre** is a measurement of **capacity**.
   b) A **kilogram** is a measurement of **capacity**.
   c) A **millilitre** is a measurement of **capacity**.

Area

area, square, rectangle, tessellation

1 Copy and complete this sentence, '**Area** means ...'.

2 Which of these shapes has the largest **area**?

 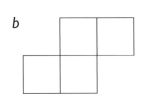 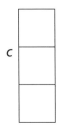

a   b   c

3 Write the names of places you know that have **area**, like 'dining area'.

4 On squared paper, draw some shapes that have an **area** of eight **squares**.

5 Which statement is true?
This **rectangle** has an area of:
a) 7 squares   b) 11 squares
c) 12 squares   d) 17 squares

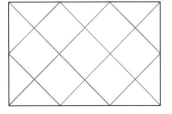

6 Find the **areas** of these three shapes.

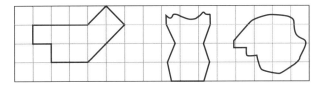

7 Find the **area** in squares of a page in your maths book.

8 Copy and complete this sentence, '**Tessellation** is ...'.

9 Look for **tessellations** around you and draw them.

10 Which of these shapes **tessellate**?
square   rectangle   triangle   circle
Draw some examples of those that tessellate.

3 Angles

angle, right-angle, half turn, quarter turn, straight angle, clockwise, anticlockwise, compass

1 Copy and complete this sentence, 'An **angle** is ...'.

2 How many **right-angles** can you see in this pattern?

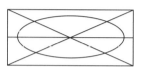

3 Which statement is true?
   a) A **half turn** is a **right-angle**.
   b) A **quarter turn** is a **right-angle**.

4 Look around your classroom. How many different **right-angles** can you see?

5 Which of these **angles** is a **straight angle**?

 *a*   *b*   *c*

6 A spinner is facing the letter N. It turns **clockwise** through one **right-angle**. Which letter is it facing now?

7 A spinner is facing the letter N. It turns **anticlockwise** through one **right-angle**. Which letter is it facing now?

8 Copy and complete this sentence, 'The four main points of a **compass** are ...'.

9 Look at this grid. Start at K and follow the instructions. Go 1 square north. **Turn clockwise** through one **right-angle**. Go 1 square east. Turn **anticlockwise** through one right-angle. Go 2 squares north. Stop. Where did you end up?

A	B	C
D	E	F
G	H	I
J	K	L

10 Using squared paper, make up a route across the paper, from one corner to another, like the one above. Give it to a friend to try.

Transformations and coordinates

reflection, line of symmetry, square, vertical, horizontal, diagonal, axis, reflection, triangle

3

1 Copy this picture and draw the **reflection** of the shape in the mirror line.

2 Which of these pictures shows a **reflection** of this pattern?

a 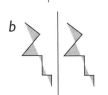   b   c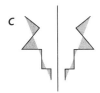

3 What is a **line of symmetry**?

4 How many **lines of symmetry** does a **square** have?

5 Colour a pattern on squared paper that has one **line of symmetry**. Is your line **vertical**, **horizontal** or **diagonal**?

6 Write down four things with more than one **line of symmetry**.

7 Using the letters on one **axis** and the numbers on the other axis, say where these things are: star, finger, heart, aeroplane, phone. The first one has been done for you: pencil – A5.

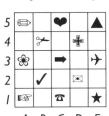

8 Draw a grid of your own with numbers on the **vertical axis** and letters on the **horizontal** axis. Draw some pictures in your grid and make up some questions.

9 Draw a **square**. Can you make these shapes by making a **reflection** with a mirror?

10 Draw a **triangle**. See how many different shapes can be found by making a **reflection** with a mirror.

Data handling

data, pictogram, tally chart, total, frequency table, Venn diagram, Carroll diagram, block graph

1 Copy and complete this sentence, '**Data** is ...'.

2 In this **pictogram** [≡] counts for two letters. Write down how many letters Jane got each day.

3 How would the **pictogram** show five letters?

4 Draw a **tally chart** showing the **data** about Jane's letters.

5 What is the **total** number of letters Jane received in this week?

6 What is a **frequency table**?

Monday:	≡ ≡
Tuesday:	≡
Wednesday:	≡ ≡ ≡
Thursday:	≡
Friday:	≡ ≡
Saturday:	≡
Sunday:	

7 Sort the numbers from 1 to 10 and complete this **Venn diagram**.

Even numbers   Numbers less than 5

8 Sort the numbers from 1 to 10 and complete this **Carroll diagram**.

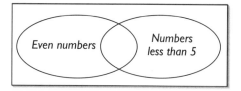

	Even numbers	Odd numbers
Numbers less than 5		
Numbers more than 5		

9 Ask the children in your class how many brothers and sisters they have. Use a **tally chart** to collect this **data** and draw a **block graph** of it.

10 Write four sentences about the **block graph** you have drawn. What does it tell you about the children in your class?

Probability

impossible, possible, certain, odd number, even number

1 Copy and complete this sentence, '**Impossible** means ...'.

2 Are these things **possible** or **impossible**?
   a) Your teacher will turn into an elephant.
   b) Your teacher will tell someone off today.
   c) Your teacher will fly to the moon at lunchtime.

3 Write some things about yourself and say whether they are **possible** or **impossible**.

4 What does the word **certain** mean?

5 Write three things that are **certain** to happen.

6 Look at a calendar. Are these things **certain**, **possible** or **impossible**?
   a) January 27th will come the day after January 26th.
   b) Christmas day will come on the day after December 26th.
   c) The day after February 28th will be February 29th.

7 Look at a dice. Write down all the **possible** numbers you can throw. Can you be **certain** to roll any of the numbers? Which numbers is it **impossible** to roll?

8 Is it **possible** to get an **odd number** from adding together two **even numbers**? Give one or two examples if you can.

9 Is it **possible** to get an **even number** from adding together two **odd numbers**? Give one or two examples if you can.

10 Find out what types of numbers you get if you add or subtract **odd** or **even numbers**.

| even + even = | odd + odd = | even + odd = | odd + even = |
| even – even = | odd – odd = | even – odd = | odd – even = |

Properties of number

digit, number, numeral, natural number, whole number, fraction, decimal, number line, alternate, consecutive, sum, sequence, century, centimetre, metre, positive number, negative number

1 Copy and complete this sentence: 'A **digit** is...'.

2 Write the **number** 'three hundred and twelve' as a **numeral**.

3 Which statement is true?
   a) a half is a **natural number**   **b)** a half is a **whole number**
   c) a half is a **fraction** of a **number**

4 Sort these **numbers** into **whole numbers**, **fractions** and **decimals**.

4	1.82	$\frac{6}{2}$	7.296	$\frac{7}{8}$	5.2	6	5.1	$\frac{3}{4}$	5000	822	$\frac{7}{100}$

5 Draw a **number line** showing numbers from 0 to 10.
   Starting at 1, mark the **alternate numbers** in red. What do we call the **numbers** you have coloured?

6 Here is a list of three **consecutive numbers**: 1, 2, 3
   Double the middle number. Find the **sum** of the first and last numbers. What do you notice?

7 Write three other **consecutive numbers** and try this again. What do you notice? Does it always work?

8 Continue this **sequence**: 1, −1, 2, −2, 3, −3, ...
   Write a sequence of your own and describe it in words.

9 How many years are there in a **century**? What do you think 'cent' stands for? Think of the word **centimetre**. How many centimetres are there in one **metre**?

10 Use a **number line** which has **positive** and **negative numbers** and follow this **number** chain.

Start on zero	+6	−3	+2	−5	−4	+1	−3	+7

   Where do you end up? Write a number chain of your own.

Place value and ordering

value, number, numeral, digit, approximation, rounding, column, whole number, decimal, tenth, unit, hundredth, equivalent, sum, minus, difference, decimal point

1 What is the **value** of the 7 in 723?

2 What **number** would you need to subtract to change the **numeral** 385 into 305?

3 Write five three-**digit numbers** that are between 400 and 500.

4 Copy and continue this pattern: 9 + 4 = 13
                                                19 + 4 = ...
                                                29 + 4 = ...
   Make up a similar pattern of your own, adding an extra tens **digit** each time.

5 Make an **approximation** by **rounding** these numbers to the nearest 100.
   490   410   234   569   888   253

6 Draw two **columns** and sort these **numbers** into **whole numbers** and **decimals**.

7	0.5	52	0.7	0	0.323	42	0.23	18	100

7 Which of the **digits** in this **number** is the **tenths digit**?
   485.27

8 Which statement is true? Three **units** and seven **hundredths** is:
   a) **equivalent** to 3.7   b) **equivalent** to 3.07
   c) **equivalent** to 30.7   d) **equivalent** to 703

9 Do these quickly:
   a) find the **sum** of 1000 and 9   b) 1010 **minus** 1
   c) find the **difference** between 3999 and 4001 d) 9990 subtract 1

10 What **numbers** can you make with these **digits** and a **decimal point**? [3] [2] [6] [5] [.]

   Write them in order, with the smallest number first.

Addition and subtraction

addition, sum, subtraction, difference, operation, inverse operation, minus, total, value

4

1 Which of these words could mean **addition**?

   plus   times   take away   sum   subtract   share   add

2 In which questions would you use **addition** to find the answer?

   a) Ric went swimming 4 times and Jon went swimming 5 times.
   How many times did they go swimming altogether?
   b) What is the **sum** of 13 and 15?
   c) Jo had 13 stamps. She lost 4. How many does she have left?

3 Which of these words mean **subtraction**?

   plus   times   take away   sum   subtract   difference   minus

4 In which questions would you use **subtraction** to find the answer?

   a) Jack had 5 sweets and Molly had 7 sweets. How many sweets
   did they have altogether?
   b) What is the **difference** between 13 and 15?
   c) Pat had 7 sweets. He gave 3 to Ben. How many did he have
   left?

5 What does the word **operation** mean in maths?

6 What is the **inverse operation** of addition?

7 Find the answers:

   a) 23 **minus** 8   **b)** the **difference** between 75 and 45
   c) the **total** of 25 and 60   **d)** the **sum** of 3 and 9

8 In each question, find the **value** of two secret numbers:

   a) the **sum** of these two numbers is 12 , their **difference** is 4
   b) if we subtract one number from the other, the answer is 12,
   their **total** is 20

9 Make up four questions of your own. Use some of these words:

   plus   take away   sum   subtract   add   difference   minus   total

10 Make up some questions that give the answer 50.

Multiplication and division

multiplication, division, sum, operation, inverse operation, division, value, plus, product

4

1 Which of these words could mean **multiplication**?
  lots of   minus   sum   multiplied by   groups of   plus   times   share

2 In which questions would you use **division** to find the answer?

> **a)** What is the **sum** of 13 and 15?
> **b)** David and Neil won £12. If they split this equally, how much would each get?
> **c)** Gary lost 3 of his stamps. He had 8 left. How many did he start with?

3 Which of these words could mean **division**?
  lots of   minus   divided by   plus   times   share   groups of

4 What does the word **operation** mean in maths? Give four examples of operations.

5 What is the **inverse operation** of **division**?

6 In each question, find the **value** of two secret numbers:
  a) one number **plus** the other number equals 7, one number times the other number equals 10
  b) the **sum** of these two numbers is 10, their **product** is 25

7 Make up four questions of your own. Use some of these words:
  plus   divide   sum   times   add   product   minus   total

8 Make up some **multiplication** questions that give the answer 24.

9 In which of these questions would you multiply to find the answer?

> **a)** Dinesh played football 3 times and Tim played football 4 times. How many times did they play football altogether?
> **b)** What is the **product** of 5 and 15?
> **c)** Sunil had 8 sweets which he shared equally with Sue. How many did he have left?

10 Make up some **division** questions that give the answer 8.

Fractions

fraction, quarter, third, sixth, half, whole number, mixed number, top-heavy fraction, improper fraction, convert, equals, number line

1 Write these **fractions** using numbers:
  a) one **quarter**   **b)** one **third**   **c)** one **sixth**

2 Draw some rectangles in your book. Colour in a **quarter** of each of them. Make them all look different. What **fraction** is not coloured in each rectangle?

3 Find a **half** of each of these **whole numbers**.
  16   20   24   30   3   15

4 What is a **quarter** of these **whole numbers**?
  16   20   24   10

5 What is a **mixed number**? Write $\frac{5}{2}$ and $\frac{7}{4}$ as mixed numbers.

6 What are **top-heavy fractions**? Find another name for these.
  Write $1\frac{1}{2}$ as a top-heavy fraction.

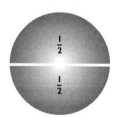 

7 Write down five **mixed numbers** and then **convert** them to **improper fractions**.

8 Which statements are true?
  a) $\frac{2}{8}$ **equals** $\frac{1}{4}$ **b)** $\frac{6}{8}$ **equals** $\frac{1}{2}$ **c)** $\frac{2}{10}$ **equals** $\frac{1}{5}$
  d) $\frac{3}{4}$ **equals** $\frac{6}{8}$ **e)** $\frac{2}{6}$ **equals** $\frac{1}{3}$

9 Write some **fractions** that are larger than $\frac{1}{2}$.

10 Draw a **number line**, like this one and mark on these **fractions**: $\frac{1}{2}$ $\frac{1}{4}$ $\frac{3}{4}$ $\frac{1}{8}$

  0   1

Decimals

digit, quarter, fraction, decimal, decimal place, hundredth, column, convert, recurring decimal

1 **a)** What does the **digit** 3 in 0.31 stand for?
b) What does the **digit** 1 in 0.31 stand for?

2 Write a **quarter** as a **fraction** and as a **decimal**.

3 How many decimal places do each of these numbers have?
2.1   0.9   4.87   8.06   12.

4 Write a number with a 4 in the **hundredths column**.

5 **Convert** these **fractions** into **decimals**:
$\frac{1}{10}$ $\frac{4}{10}$ $\frac{1}{2}$ $\frac{1}{100}$ $\frac{13}{100}$

6 Write two examples of **recurring decimals**.

7 What **fraction** of crosses are in the ring?
Write your answer as a **decimal**.
Write the fraction of crosses outside the ring as a decimal.

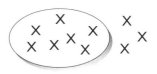

8 Draw four circles. Draw ten crosses for each one, some inside and some outside the circle. Write as a decimal the **fraction** of crosses inside the circle and the fraction of crosses outside the circle.

9 Which statements are true?
a) 0.25 equals $\frac{1}{4}$ **b)** $\frac{6}{8}$ equals 0.25   **c)** 0.2 equals $\frac{1}{5}$
d) $\frac{3}{4}$ equals 0.34   **e)** $0.\dot{3}$ equals $\frac{1}{3}$

10 Write some true and false sentences of your own about **decimals**. Now write whether they are true or false.

Number patterns and algebra

sequence, rectangular number, square number, numeral, difference, number, factor, number line, alternate, consecutive, whole number

1 Continue this **sequence**:   1, 4, 7, 10, 13, ...

2 What are **rectangular numbers**? Give some examples.

3 Which of these sets of buttons show **square numbers**?

a   b   c   d   e

Draw some more square numbers and write them as **numerals**.

4 1, 4, 9, 16, 25. What are these **numbers** called?
Find the **difference** between the numbers in this **sequence**.

5 Choose a **square number**, like 25. Find all the **factors**.
How many factors are there? Find all the factors of other square numbers. What do you notice?

6 Draw a **number line** from 0 to 10. Starting at 1 mark the **alternate numbers** in red. What do we call these numbers?

7 What does the word **consecutive** mean? Write four consecutive **whole numbers**. Can you find a quick way of adding them together?

8 The rule for finding the next **number** in this **sequence** is 'multiply by 3 and subtract 1'. Find the next three numbers in this sequence: 1, 2, ...

9 Find the **values** of the numbers being described:
   a) I think of a **number**, when I add four to it, I get 10.
   b) I think of a **number**, when I multiply by 2, I get 10.
   c) I think of a **number**, when I divide by 2, I get 10.
   d) I think of a **number**, when I subtract 14, I get 10.

10 Make up some riddles of your own for your friends to try.

Names of two-dimensional shapes

rectangle, oblong, quadrilateral, circle, square, two-dimensional, polygon, regular, equilateral triangle, isosceles triangle, irregular, oval

1 What is the difference between a **rectangle** and an **oblong**?

2 What does the word **quadrilateral** mean?
   Write the names of two different types.

3 Why are **rectangles**, **circles** and **squares** called **two-dimensional** shapes?

4 Copy and complete this sentence, 'A **polygon** is ...'.

5 Choose the correct name for each shape from the names in the box.

pentagon	hexagon	heptagon	octagon

   a   b   c   d

6 Which of the shapes in question five is a **regular polygon**?

7 Draw an **equilateral triangle** and an **isosceles triangle**.
   Write the correct name under each one.

8 Which of these **polygon** shapes do you see as road signs?
   Write down the names of these polygons and draw them.

9 Draw two different **irregular polygons**. What makes them irregular?

10 What is the difference between an **oval** and a **circle**?

4 Properties of two-dimensional shapes

base, heptagon, vertex, reflective symmetry, line of symmetry, isosceles triangle, triangle, apex, decagon, perimeter, right-angled triangle, right-angle, Venn diagram, polygon, area

1 Copy and complete this sentence, 'The **base** of a shape is ...'.

2 Draw a **heptagon** and mark on a **vertex**. How many vertices does a heptagon have?

3 Which shapes have **reflective symmetry**?

a b c d

4 How many **lines of symmetry** do these shapes have?

a b c

5 Draw some shapes which have:
   a) no **lines of symmetry**   **b)** two **lines of symmetry**
   c) four **lines of symmetry**

6 Draw an **isosceles triangle**. Mark the **base** of the **triangle** in blue and the **apex** of the triangle in red.

7 True or false?
   a) a **decagon** has six sides
   b) the **perimeter** of a shape is the space inside it
   c) a **right-angled triangle** has two **right-angles**

8 Copy and complete this **Venn diagram**, using the shapes given:

   triangle   rectangle
   oval   pentagon
   square   octagon
   circle   semicircle

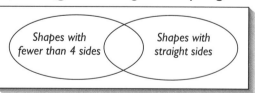

9 In which of these **polygons** is the **base** the longest side?

a b c

10 Which of the shapes in question nine has the largest **area**?

Circles

diameter, radius, circle, centimetre, millimetre, perimeter, circumference, line of symmetry, ellipse, reflective symmetry, base, cylinder, sphere, cone, pyramid, quadrant, right-angle, rotation, turn

4

1 Copy and complete this sentence, 'A **diameter** is ...'.

2 Draw round a circular lid and mark on the **radius** and **diameter** of the **circle**. Measure these lines carefully using **centimetres** and **millimetres**. What do you notice about these numbers?

3 What is the special name for the **perimeter** of a **circle**?

4 Draw another **circle** and mark on the **circumference**. Use string to measure the circumference.

5 How many **lines of symmetry** does an **ellipse** have?

6 Which of these shapes have **reflective symmetry**?

a   b   c   d

7 True or false?
   a) The **base** of a **cylinder** is a **circle**.
   b) The **base** of a **sphere** is a **circle**.
   c) The **base** of a **cone** is a **circle**.
   d) The **base** of a **pyramid** is a **circle**.

8 Draw a **quadrant** of a **circle**. Mark on any **right-angles** you can see.

9 If you made a complete **rotation**, how many **right-angles** would you **turn** through?

10 Why do you think **circles** and **cylinders** are used as wheels and for gears inside machinery? What is special about a circle?

Names of three-dimensional shapes

cube, cuboid, prism, three-dimensional, two-dimensional, tetrahedron, solid shape, hemisphere, sphere, face

1 What is the difference between a **cube** and a **cuboid**?

2 What is another name for a **cuboid**?

3 Draw a picture of two different types of **prism**. Write what types of prism you have drawn.

4 Write the names of some **three-dimensional** shapes. Pick one of them to draw and write its name underneath. Why are these shapes called three-dimensional?

5 Write the names of some **two-dimensional** shapes. Why are they called two-dimensional?

6 Draw a picture of a **tetrahedron**. What is special about a tetrahedron?

7 Unscramble the names of these **solid shapes** and join the letters of the shapes to the correct names.

onec   oehttarenrd   phimreeseh   preesh   idbouc

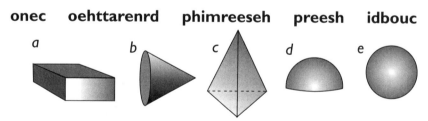

8 How many **hemispheres** are needed to make a **sphere**?

9 Copy and complete this sentence, 'Another name for a three-dimensional shape is ...'. Write the names of some shapes that are not three-dimensional.

10 Write the number of **faces** for each of the shapes in question seven.

Properties of three-dimensional shapes

edge, face, cube, solid shape, cuboid, Venn diagram, three-dimensional, cone, rectangular prism, circular prism

1   Copy and complete this sentence, 'An **edge** of a shape is ...'.

2   Copy and complete this sentence, 'A **face** of a shape is ...'.

3   Draw a picture of a **cube**. Draw two arrows to show an **edge** and a **face**.

4   How many **faces** and **edges** do these shapes have? Get some **solid shapes** to help you.

      cuboid   sphere   cylinder   cube

Find shapes around you like boxes and cans. How many **faces** and **edges** do they have?

5   What do you notice about the **faces** and **edges** of a **cube** and a **cuboid**?

6   Copy this **Venn diagram** and put the shapes in question four into the correct places. Get some **three-dimensional** shapes to help you.

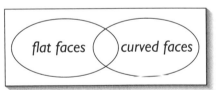

7   True or false?
    a) a **cuboid** has six **faces**   b) a **cube** has six **edges**
    c) **solid shapes** are **three-dimensional**

8   Draw a **cone**. How many **faces** and **edges** does it have?

9   Get some triangular paper.
    Try drawing some **cubes** and
    cuboids on it, like the one shown.

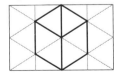

10   Another name for a **cuboid** is a **rectangular prism**.
    What is another name for a **circular prism**?

4 Length

perimeter, centimetre, millimetre, kilogram, metre, circle, diameter, radius, rectangle, base, height, length, scale

I   Copy and complete this sentence, '**Perimeter** means ...'.

2   Find the **perimeter** of these shapes in **centimetres**.

a   b   c

3   Which of these lines is 50 **millimetres** long?

a _____   b _____

c _____

4   Which statements are true?
   a) 3cm means 3 **centimetres**   **b)** 6m means 6 **millimetres**
   c) 14km means 14 **kilograms**   **d)** 28m means 28 **metres**

5   Write these measurements in three ways. The first one has been done for you.

millimetres	centimetres and millimetres	centimetres
52mm	5cm and 2mm	5.2cm
84mm		
71mm		

6   Draw a **circle** and mark on the **diameter** and **radius**. Measure these lines carefully using **centimetres** and **millimetres**.

7   What is the special name for the **perimeter** of a **circle**?

8   How many **millimetres** make up one **centimetre**?

9   This pattern is made from **rectangles**. Measure the **base** and **height** of each one and write down its **perimeter**.

10 Find instruments used to measure **length**, such as a ruler, metre stick, tape measure, etc. Look at the **scale** marked on each. Do they show **centimetres**, **millimetres** or **metres**?

Time

rotation, turn, century, half, quarter, millennium, time, twenty-four-hour clock, a.m., p.m., clockwise, multiplication

4

1 What does **rotation** mean?

2 How long does it take the minute hand on a clock to **turn** a complete **rotation**?

3 How many years are there in:
a) a **century**? b) **half** a **century**? c) **quarter** of a **century**?

4 True or false?
a) A **millennium** is 100 years.
b) A **millennium** is 2000 years.
c) A **millennium** is a day in the year 2000.
d) A **millennium** is 1000 years.

5 What **time** does this clock show? How would you show this time on a **twenty-four-hour** clock?

6 What do **a.m.** and **p.m.** mean?

7 Write down what you are usually doing at these **times** on a school day:

7.15 **a.m.**	3.15 **p.m.**	8.45 **a.m.**
7.30 **p.m.**	12.30 **p.m.**	1.00 **a.m.**

8 A clock shows this **time**:
What time will the clock show if the minute hand moves a **quarter** of a **rotation clockwise**? Write your answer in words and as a digital time on a **twenty-four-hour clock**.

9 How many complete **rotations** will the minute hand make in one day?

10 There are 365 days in a normal year. Using **multiplication**, find out roughly how many days old you are.

4 Mass and capacity

mass, scales, scale, convert, grams, kilograms, capacity, litre, imperial units, millilitre

1 What is **mass**?

2 Which statement is true?
   a) 100 g equals 1 kg   **b)** 14 kg means 14 kilograms
   c) 28 litres means 28 metres

3 Mrs Smith is standing on her bathroom **scales**.
Read the **scale** to see how much she weighs.

4 **Convert** these **grams** to **kilograms**:

grams	kilograms
1500	
3600	
7000	
500	

5 A carton of orange juice weighs about:
   a) 1 **kilogram**   **b)** 10 **kilograms**   **c)** 100 **kilograms**

6 Write three things you would measure in **grams**.
Write three things you would measure in **kilograms**.

7 What does **capacity** measure?

8 The **capacity** of a kettle is about:
   a) $1\frac{1}{2}$ **litres**   **b)** 15 **litres**   **c)** 150 **litres**

9 Write the names of some **imperial units** of **capacity**.

10 Write three things you would measure in **litres**.
Write three things you would measure in **millilitres**.

Area

area, quadrilateral, square centimetre, rectangle, length, base, height, circle, square

I Copy and complete this sentence, '**Area** means ...'.

2 What is the **area** in squares of these **quadrilaterals**?

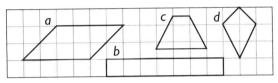

3 On squared paper, draw four different **quadrilaterals** with an **area** of four squares.

4 Copy and complete this sentence, 'A **square centimetre** is ...'.

5 Which of these abbreviations is a shorter way of writing **square centimetre**?   cm   sc   cm2 cm^2

6 Draw these **rectangles** on to squared paper. The **lengths** of the sides are given. Use the shapes to find the areas in cm^2.

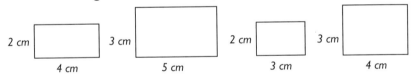

7 Write down how you can find the **area** of a **rectangle** using multiplication.

8 Using multiplication, find the **areas** of these **rectangles** in cm^2.

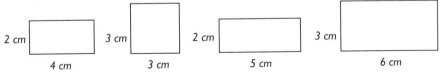

9 Draw three **rectangles** of different sizes. Measure the **base** and **height** of the rectangles and write down the **area** of each of them.

10 Using squared paper, try to find the **area** of a **circle** by counting **squares** and part squares.

Angles

4

angle measurer, symbol, degree, straight angle, turn, rotation, right-angle, clockwise, anticlockwise, compasses, compass, horizontal, vertical

1 Copy and complete this sentence, 'An **angle measurer** is ...'.

2 What **symbol** do we use to show **degrees**?

3 How many **degrees** are there in:
   a) a **straight angle**   **b)** a full **turn**

4 Which statements are true?
   a) There are two **straight angles** in a full **turn**.
   b) There are 90° in a full **turn**.
   c) Another name for a **turn** is a **rotation**.

5 Use an **angle measurer** to measure **right-angles** in your classroom.

6 A spinner is facing the letter N.
   It **turns clockwise** through one and a half **rotations**.
   Which letter is it facing now?

7 A spinner is facing the letter N. It turns **anticlockwise** through three and a quarter **rotations**. Which letter is it facing now?

8 Draw a circle using a pair of **compasses**.
   Mark on it eight points of the **compass**.

9 Is Pauline or Iain telling the truth?

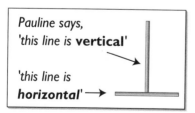

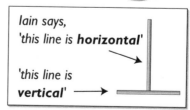

10 Draw a picture of a house. Colour the **horizontal** lines in red and the **vertical** lines in blue.

Transformations and coordinates

transformation, translation, rotation, half, reflection, reflective symmetry, coordinates, ordered pair, axis, vertical, horizontal

1 Copy and complete this sentence: 'A **transformation** is ...'.

2 What are the four main types of **transformations**?

3 Which statement is true? A **translation** changes a shape:
   a) by enlarging it   **b)** by sliding it   **c)** by turning it

4 Which picture shows a **rotation**? Which **transformations** do the others show?

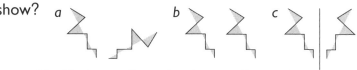

5 Draw a picture of **half** a butterfly and colour it. Draw the **reflection** to make the butterfly have **reflective symmetry**.

6 Copy and complete this sentence, '**Coordinates** are ...'.

7 Look at the grid below. Write down the **coordinates** for the points A, B, C, D as **ordered pairs**.

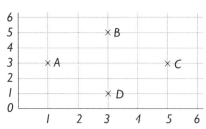

8 Using squared paper, draw a grid with numbers from 0 to 12 and label the x **axis** and y axis. Which axis is the **vertical** axis? Which is the **horizontal** axis?

9 Plot these **ordered pairs** on to your grid and join them up.
   (8, 9) (6, 9) (5, 8) (5, 6) (4, 6) (4, 8) (2, 8) (2, 6) (1, 6) (1, 9) (0, 8)
   (0, 9) (1, 10) (5, 10) (7, 12) (7, 11) (8, 10) (8, 9)
   What have you drawn?

10 Draw a simple picture on a new grid and carefully write the **coordinates** in order. Give the coordinates to your friends to see if they can guess what it is!

4 Data handling

axis, bar chart, graph, vertical, horizontal, data, bar-line graph, tally chart, set, number, median, mode, scale

1 What does the word **axis** mean?

2 Look at this **bar chart**. What is this **graph** showing?

3 What does the **vertical axis** show? What about the **horizontal** axis?

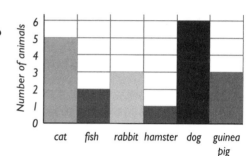

4 Draw this same **data** on to a **bar-line graph**.

5 How many dogs are marked on the **bar chart**?

6 Which **tally chart** shows the same information as the **bar chart**?

a
cat	ⅡⅡ Ⅱ
fish	I I
rabbit	I I I
hamster	
dog	ⅡⅡ Ⅱ
guinea pig	I I

b
cat	ⅡⅡ Ⅱ
fish	I
rabbit	I I
hamster	I I I
dog	ⅡⅡ Ⅱ
guinea pig	I

c
cat	ⅡⅡ Ⅱ
fish	I I
rabbit	I I I
hamster	I
dog	ⅡⅡ Ⅱ I
guinea pig	I I I

7 Look at this **set** of **numbers**: What is the **median** of these numbers? What is the **mode** of these numbers?

1 2 5 7 7 9 11 11 11 12 12

8 Write a **set** of five **numbers** with a **median** of six.

9 Ask the children in your class what type of pets they have. Use a **tally chart** to collect this **data** and draw a **bar chart** of it.

10 Write four sentences about the **bar chart** you have drawn. Which is the most popular pet? What **scale** have you used on your **vertical axis**?

Probability

equally likely outcomes, possible, outcome, certain, impossible, even number, odd number, number

1 What are **equally likely outcomes**?

2 On a dice, how many **equally likely outcomes** are there?
Write down all the **possible outcomes** you can roll.

3 Are these things **certain**, **possible** or **impossible**?
a) Saturday will be the day after Sunday **b)** it will rain tomorrow
c) 2 + 2 will equal 4

4 Write some stories of your own and say whether they are
certain, **possible** or **impossible**.

5 Look at this spinner and answer these questions:
a) How many **equally likely outcomes** are there?
b) Is it **certain**, **possible** or **impossible** to spin
an even number?
c) How many **outcomes** are there that give
an **odd number**?
d) Is it **certain**, **possible** or **impossible** to spin a 7?

6 Is this statement true?
It is **impossible** to pick the Queen of Hearts from a complete
pack of playing cards, without looking.

7 How many **equally likely outcomes** are there when picking a
card from a complete pack of cards?

8 Find out what types of **numbers** you get if you multiply **odd** or
even numbers.
even × even =   odd × odd =   even × odd =   odd × even =

9 Is it **possible** to get an **even number** from multiplying two
odd numbers? Give one or two examples if you can.

10 Is it **possible** to get an **odd number** from multiplying two
even numbers? Give one or two examples if you can.